PHANTOM PAINS OF MADNESS

Noelle

Kocot

Phantom

Pains

of

Madness

Wave

Books

Seattle

&

New

York

Published by Wave Books

www.wavepoetry.com

Wave Books titles are distributed to the trade by

Consortium Book Sales and Distribution

Phone: 800-283-3572 / SAN 631-760X

Library of Congress Cataloging-in-Publication Data'

Kocot, Noelle.

[Poems. Selections]

Phantom pains of madness / Noelle Kocot. — First edition.

pages ; cm

ISBN 978-1-940696-25-6 (limited edition hardcover)

ISBN 978-1-940696-30-0 (softcover)

I. Title.

PS3611.O36A6 2016

811'.6—dc23

2015025696

Designed and composed by Quemadura

Printed in the United States of America

9 8 7 6 5 4 3 2 1

First Edition

Wave Books 056

For
Charlie
Wright
and
his
family

PHANTOM PAINS OF MADNESS

The

Squeegee

Looks

Peculiar

In

This

December

Light

I

Am

Chewing

On

A

Cuticle

I

Have

Become

Adept

At

Perseverance

A

Jewel

On

A

Blank

Canvas

You

Have

Changed

Forms

So

What

The

Hell

Is

That

Supposed

To

Mean

To

Me

With

Your

Appeal

Of

Disorder

And

A

Winding–

Sheet

And

I

Don't

Know

How

To

Feel

But

I'll

Just

Go

Ahead

And

Take

This

Pill

And

Then

I'll

Be

As

Right

As

The

Soft

Winter

Rain

And

The

Little

Legs

Of

Freedom

Walked

On

While

You

Stood

Still

And

Worried

How

Can

Breath

Be

Sliced

Or

Pounce

Like

Malarkey

You

Are

Tangled

In

Languors

And

You

Don't

Obfuscate

The

Neon

Wires

In

Your

Brain

So

Filled

With

Pulchritude

And

Peopleness

And

The

Detritus

Of

Your

Instincts

In

That

Zone

Bears

The

Contour

Of

Being

As

Literal

As

We

Possibly

Are

That

Moon

Hangs

In

The

Sky

Like

A

Drop

Of

Dough

And

The

Sharking

Ribs

Of

Stars

Tell

It

What

They

See

And

You

My

Friend

Have

Suffered

And

Are

Congruous

&

Condensed

And

Your

Handsome

Green

Purring

Is

Only

The

Radiator's

Heat

And

I

Go

On

With

My

Breast

Strokes

To

The

Kitchen

Where

Evening

Breathes

Violinists

Will

Tell

You

Just

How

The

Dawn

Breaks

And

That

Dusky

House

Filled

With

Its

Tonights

Is

Slow

And

Beautiful

But

I

Have

Polio

You

Said

To

Me

Once

As

The

Hunks

Of

Ice

Streamed

Down

A

Gravitational

Field

One

Shrug

One

Suitcase

These

Clothes

That

Will

Outlast

Me

Surfing

The

Shield

Of

Pathetic

The

Aureole

Of

A

Little

Song

Without

The

Music

I

Am

Telling

You

The

Truth

That

The

Limitations

Were

All

Pure

Lies

The

Jupiters

And

The

Saturns

Turn

Likewise

We

Are

Heavy

Ancient

To

The

Fountain

We

Are

Most

Grateful

Who

Can

Afford

This

Celestial

Spectacle

Our

Pockets

Are

Empty

But

We

Are

Black-

Fired

And

Burning

The

Past's

Relinquishment

A

Fog

That

Is

Created

In

Silence

A

Word

Stripped

Of

Its

Symbol

Turning

Again

And

Again

And

Here

My

Final

Invisible

Sentence

Ceases

To

Begin

Each

Suffix

Tied

To

The

Masses

That

Roam

And

Roam

They

Steal

A

Hearse

Waiting

For

The

New

Boy

To

Arrive

But

Tonight

At

A

Bookstore

We've

Got

To

Make

Some

Corrections

To

Our

Scale

That

Puppet

On

The

Lamp

Says

We

Must

We

Must

And

The

Empty

Bucket

By

Our

Bed

Is

A

Source

Of

Patience

An

Emotion

Floating

Above

Our

Feelings

O

This

Is

All

So

Pretty

That

I

Think

Now

I

Will

Swallow

A

Locust

And

Maybe

Even

A

Plus

Sign

Center

Beginning

To

Form

In

The

Deciduous

Light

Somewhere

In

This

Room

A

Little

Brilliant

Morpheme

Gaudy

And

Even

Stern

It

Points

Toward

The

Skin

Of

Heaven

And

We

Are

Left

Words

Within

Words

Our

Vertical

Miseries

&

Joys

A

Hereafter

Where

Infinite

Hope

The

Most

Profound

Kind

Lays

Itself

Out

An

Assertion

Of

Afterlife

Or

Maybe

Just

The

Lonely

Unheard

Of

Young

Falconer's

Ruined

Face

Turned

Upward

To
The
Great
Empty
Sky

Lovers

Unreal

Grace

The

Pavement

We

Must

Shield

Our

Eyes

From

Their

Radiance

Howls

And

Yowls

And

Aftermath

Of

Solids

Gutted

And

Flayed

And

Laid

Out

The

Power

Of

Equals

Relentless

As

Collision's

Verbs

I

Must

See

This

For

Myself

That

It

Is

Not

Us

Crumbling

As

We

Wait

For

The

Sky's

Mind

To

Bury

Us

In

Its

Medieval

Teeth

Death

Instinct

With

Me

Since

At

Least

Birth

So

Interwoven

With

The

Fabric

Of

My

Being

Gone

Gone

Between

2

Weeks

Ago

And

Last

Week

Only

Life

Is

Left

And

It

Is

Precious

All

Internalized

Self–

Hatred

Gone

(Remember

It's

The

Imago

Not

The

Person

As

They

Stand

In

The

Creator's

Eyes)

I

Am

Not

An

Ogre

And

Without

All

Of

This

Propelling

Me

To

Write

Poems

What

Is

Left

Only

The

Life

The

Singing

Language

Around

The

Life

I

Don't

Know

The

Future

But

Exile

And

Mitosis

Are

The

Commas

That

Lurch

Us

Into

A

Galaxy

Of

Forever

And

The

Fluency

Of

Rhetoric

And

Anachronistic

Blood

Wear

The

Face

Of

Adrenaline

Fists

Which

Punch

Out

Into

Frustration

And

The

Worth

Of

The

Plan

And

The
Fruit
That
It
Bears

Frailty

Of

Strabismus

How

Could

You

Know

The

Orange

Light

On

Fire

With

The

Minutiae

Of

The

Day

Belonged

To

You

And

You

Only

And

That

This

Pain

Of

Years

Was

A

Keepsake

You

Held

In

Your

Red

Heart

For

All

To

See

Beyond

Your

Frailty

And

A

Message

To

The

One

And

Only

Sun?

Tainted

Black

Prairie

Soaked

In

Oils

How

Can

I

"Describe"

You

How

Can

I

Define

You

Rubbery

With

Authentic

Fascination

It

Is

A

Holy

Feeling

Somehow

This

Freedom

And

Now

We're

All

Together

And

The

Moles

On

Our

Shoulders

Go

All

Punk

Rock

And

Smiling

Crazy

Maybe

But

Still

In

The

Heart

Of

The

Quietude

This

Unity

This

Blessing

These

Words

That

Weigh

Almost

Nothing

They

Merge

They

Gel

They

Intoxicate—

Why

Do

I

Piously

Accept

The

Beak

And

Mark

Of

Degrees

The

Tempest

In

The

Nests

The

Indulgence

Of

The

Sun's

Blades

Over

A

Corner

Of

A

Tablecloth

Full

Swing

Into

The

Pounding

Of

A

Heart

We

Stand

Fastened

To

A

Mirror

While

A

Slow

Tune

Rises

And

Sets

Like

The

Air

Through

A

Wave

And

Then

We

Drop

Off

To

Sleep

The

Sleep

Of

Coral

Sitting

On

Its

Side

And

Then

We

Say

This

Is

What

We

Call

Life

The

Planet

Is

Heavy

But

The

Black

Hole

Is

Near

Dear

Sister

Why

Do

You

Hide

Inside

Pink

Ice

A

Sleep-

Talking

Thought

Arises

Plainly

I'm

Miles

Away

And

Yet

The

Vibrations

Of

Your

Rest

Imprison

Me

Nightly

I

Believe

That

Possession

Only

Causes

Guilt

And

That

Destiny

Is

A

Tuning

Fork

Meant

For

Crying

Statues

I

Believe

That

I

Will

Be

Fired

For

No

Reason

From

My

Job

As

Record

Keeper

But

Only

When

My

Stem

Cells

Ripen

Fugitive

Healing

Of

Divine

Mind

So

Earthbound

And

So

Sublime

I

Kiss

You

This

Morning

In

Thanks

That

You

Tell

Me

I

Am

A

Good

Cat

Dear

Lover

The

Gravity

Of

You

Doesn't

Provoke

Doubt

From

Head

To

Tail

And

I

React

With

Some

Kindness

Of

My

Own

My

Empty

Pockets

Have

No

Holes

But

You

Stranger

You

Are

The

Existence

Of

The

Obvious

Ink

I

Expend

A

Ball

Of

Yarn

Out

In

The

Yard

Yearning

The

Day

Starts

Out

Like

A

(___)

For

Breakfast

We

Have

(___)

And

For

Lunch

We

Have

(___)

The

Inchoate

Jesting

Tongue

Survives

Like

Truth

That

Churns

In

Our

Stomachs

Doubt

And

(____)

Fill

Our

Awareness

No

We

Are

Not

Buried

In

Our

Graves

But

The

Fish

Still

Stinks

Like

(____)

A

Future

Full

Of

Holes

The

Intonations

Of

Hair

Sweeping

The

Grass

We

Are

(____)

Like

The

Word

(____)

Swaying

On

Its

Precious

Stem

It's

That

Time

Of

Day

The

Votive

Hour

Where

A

Green

Trellis

Glistens

With

Rain

And

The

Flare

Of

This

Wallpaper

Is

Dyed

Like

A

Cherry

Where

Is

My

Jewel

Case

Where

Are

The

Golden

Rusty

Leaves

That

Hang

From

A

Delicate

Gold

Chain

And

Light

The

Afternoon

Shade

With

Its

Dark

Stems

Soon

A

Boat

Will

Come

And

We

Will

Catch

Fish

For

Dinner

But

First

A

Cocktail

With

A

Small

Pink

Umbrella

Will

Sail

Unto

Us

Like

A

Virgin

Washing

Her

Round

Toes

My

Closets

Are

Bothering

Me

Today

And

The

Holy

Spirit

Drowned

In

Mud

And

The

Little

Moths

With

Their

Gray

Carpet

Coloring

This

Misuse

Of

Our

Resources

Is

Certainly

Something

To

Complain

About

Maroon

Life

Of

The

Things

That

Pass

And

The

Bloody

Sunsets

And

Tropical

Calm

The

Epistemology

Of

Husband

Tinks

Out

And

Out

It's

No

Good

To

Spend

So

Much

Time

Alone

I

Aired

Out

My

Heart

Like

A

Scumbag

That

Is

Seeing

The

Light

Of

Day

For

The

First

Time

We

All

Lose

The

Edge

Of

Our

Bodies'

Nakedness

And

The

Heart's

Inability

To

Field

Its

Own

Blood

The

Young

And

The

Old

Gently

Brush

The

Scabs

Off

The

Skin

Around

A

Breeze

While

A

Train

Cracks

In

All

Its

Splendor

The

Broken

Silences

And

A

Shadow

On

A

Canvas

Grow

Taller

Now

As

We

Bounce

Off

Revelry

An

Organ

Rifling

Through

The

Broken

Measures

And

A

Nursery

Rhyme

Is

All

Muddled

In

Its

Fragments

Who

Is

To

Say

That

The

Drawn

Skin

Underneath

The

Windows

Will

Not

Regenerate

Into

A

Garment

We

Wear

Once

And

Then

Discard

While

Pedestal

And

Broken

Legs

Wait

Right

Here

Deep

Freeze

Of

The

Unconscious

My

Mind

Drops

Its

Anchorite

But

Only

For

A

Second

It

Is

Seldom

Clear

And

Is

Delicate

And

Fraught

With

Monsters

Pushing

Themselves

Into

Some

Real

Place

The

Innards

Of

Time

And

The

Mixed

Pigments

Display

Their

Meanings

And

Flicker

In

The

Aviary

I

Wonder

If

Desire

Is

Tensile

Or

Is

It

More

"Dutiful"

Than

We

Once

Thought

Because

What

We

Thought

Was

Growing

Was

Really

An

Electric-

Blue

Lingering

Shadow

On

The

Brown

Face

Of

The

Moon

Delirium

Delivered

Of

You

As

Pink

Surrender

Washes

The

Sky

Do

You

Know

Where

Mars

Is

Nobody

Does

Really

These

Are

The

Salad

Days

She

Harangues

And

Harangues

As

Blue

Ghosts

Halo

The

Waning

Moon

Orange

Is

The

Only

Color

Not

In

The

Bible

And

A

Floral

Sunstorm

Sends

Its

Fantastic

Spray

While

We

Nod

Out

Leprosy

And

Maybe

Pancakes

Thus

We

Are

Alone

And

Sea

Monsters

Become

All

The

More

Negligible

Truth

Be

Told

This

Is

Our

Crowning

Achievement

The

Massive

Characters

Are

Seared

With

Scars

The

Blue

Foibles

That

Keep

Us

Sorry

As

A

Willow

We

Stand

Frozen

Before

Chimera

And

Lack

The

Only

Ones

Who

Matter

Anymore

Your

Silver

Linings

Ring

On

The

Horsefly
With
His
Flapjack
Wings

Not

The

Night

With

Its

Nests

That

Enhance

You

Not

The

Cakes

With

Their

Smooth

Sugars

Not

The

Black

Moon

Doling

Out

Huge

Sweeping

Pieces

Of

Your

Destiny

You

Are

Seen

This

One

Way

By

Some

And

A

Totally

Different

Way

By

Others

Just

Get

On

This

Train

And

I

Will

Explain

It

All

Until

Perhaps

Something

Desolate

Happens

On

The

Tracks

Stretching

Over

Some

Past

Some

Future

Loneliness

In

The

Diabolical

Good

Light

A

Mass

Grave

Has

Been

Found

At

A

Reform

School

And

Those

Nosebleeds

And

Razors

We

Now

Find

Had

A

Root

But

We

Didn't

Know

Before

No

We

Didn't

Know

Before

And

It

Wouldn't

Be

Difficult

To

Say

We

Don't

Know

Now

Either

If

I

Pay

You

Back

In

Kind

Our

Betrayal

Will

Become

Our

Very

Grief

And

The

Pages

Of

The

Almanac

Will

Prematurely

Yellow

Over

Love's

Fine

Weather

Muscling

Its

Way

Across

All

Our

Months

Where

We

Are

Charmed

By

How

A

Feral

Cat

Races

Over

Our

Lawn

Continually

The

Bullet

In

The

Heart

Bursts

Into

A

Flower

The

Soul

Has

Lost

Its

Verb

But

Still

Goes

Fleas

Everywhere

But

No

Dog

This

Time
This
Time
You
Are
On
Your
Own
Sir

Eggshells

Like

Bones

Lie

Crushed

In

The

Garbage

Like

Candy

Crushed

Like

The

Crushed

Toys

Of

Children

But

We

Will

Not

Speak

Of

That

Instead

We

Tune

Our

Instruments

Made

Of

Tin

Not

Bone

And

We

Touch

The

Apparition

Of

Our

Toes

Which

Are

Like

Solid

Doves

Made

Out

Of

Bone

Not

Tin

Look

At

How

That

Juice

Squeezes

Itself

Into

That

Glass

Over

There

And

How

We

Indulge

In

Our

Caresses

Until

The

Train

Helps

Us

To

Rest

By

Simply

Speeding

Off

Without

Us

The

Stars

In

The

Movies

Are

Not

The

Same

They

Touch

Briefly

Then

The

Fires

Go

Out

I

Wish

I

Could

Shake

Loose

Of

Them

But

The

Only

Thing

I

Can

Do

Is

To

Wave

My

Purple

Scarf

A

Long

Nap

Of

Thorns

A

Tidbit

Of

Garbage

Rollicking

Around

Our

Drain

Snaps

Once

Snaps

Twice

Snaps

Because

It's

Frustrated

Or

Can't

Just

Can't

Tidbit

Upon

Tidbit

All

It

Can

Do

Is

Try

To

Stop

Itself

But

It

Can't

Just

Can't

And

Offers

Instead

A

Thornless

Rose

In

Spring

It's

The

Living

Of

It

And

This

Cold

Is

Affecting

People

I

Do

Not

Mingle

At

The

Star-

Lit

Looted

Mall

But

I

Gather

My

Belongings

Like

Bread

To

My

Chest

Not

Too

Many

And

Not

Too

Dark

Anymore

Is

Different

Nowadays

It

Talks

In

Soothing

Voices

And

Never

Even

Alludes

To

The

Rack

And

The

Screw

It

Will

Hush

The

Drum

Of

A

Train

Rewinding

Read

A

Manual

For

Sock

Puppets

Not

Too

Bad

You

Say

But

Then

Again

Living

In

The

Empire

Is

Its

Own

Sorrow

Delirium

Sunlight

Teeth

Hurt

From

Chewing

Stop

Give

Back

Stop

Just

Give

There

That's

The

Way

You

Do

That

The

God–

Hunger

In

Its

Right

Place

Lord

Make

It

Not

For

Me

This

Time

Maybe

I

Is

Multiple

Symbolizing

Death

Or

Tragedy

Or

Maybe

I

Will

Get

A

Good

Laugh

Singularly

In

A

Stadium

Full

Of

Dust

That

A

Boy

In

The

World

Can

Run

His

Fingers

Over

Once

Twice

And

What

They

Named

You

Edges

Over

Your

Visual

Cliff

Going

Gone

Women

Of

A

Certain

Age

Have

Been

Initiating

Me

With

Their

Smiles

And

Kind

Eyes

And

Crossbows

Strapped

To

Their

Sagging

Arms

Tired

Shoulders

Free

Of

Their

Sirens

He

Swears

He

Can

See

A

White

Lifesaver

Off

In

The

Distance

Throw

It

To

The

Ground

My

Townspeople

Pull

Out

The

Bones

And

The

Feathers

Poorly

As

Angels

No

The

Surge

In

Our

Bodies

Inimical

Stretched

Amplified

Toy

Piano

Blurred

Across

The

Giddy

Breezes

Without

Us

Looking

On

Friend

It's

All

Right

If

You

Never

Wake

Up

Wet

Unfetterings

Edges

Of

Sleep

Edges

Of

The

Throat

Wingspan

From

Ankle

To

Mouth

Unheard

It

Is

The

Absence

Of

Scene

And

A

Filched

Mushroom

In

A

Supermarket

Will

Neither

Help

Nor

Harm

That

Head-on

Collision

Communication

Goddess

Moon

Husband

Or

I

Would

Have

Asked

You

To

Stare

And

Point

Nothing

Chilling

About

It

Anymore

Our

Common

Song

Goes

On
And
On
And
I
Find
I
Want
Ceaselessly

Everything

A

Whirl

Of

Molecules

Marathon

Hair

Evaporating

Spray

Togetherness

Threads

Pulled

A

Fast-

Moving

Object

A

Bird's

Flight

Demanding

Demanding

What

Demanding

Love

A
Light
Green
Bug
Hopping
From
Word
Into
Sun

ACKNOWLEDGMENTS

There are way too many people to name, and I'm sure I would forget some, so I'll just say that grateful acknowledgment is made to the *Brooklyn Rail*, where some of these poems were published, Charlie and Barb Wright and the late Bagley Wright, Joshua Beckman (beautiful poet and my editor), Matthew Zapruder, Matt Rohrer, Anthony McCann, and Mary Ruefle (beautiful poets), Heidi Broadhead, Brittany Dennison, Blyss Ervin, and the rest of the Wave Books staff, David Caligiuri, Damon Tomblin, Lizzette Potthoff, Paul Vlachos, my dear parents Jo-Ann and Jack Sleight, Curtis McCartney, Cindy Cuarino, Monica Antolik, Isaac ben Ayala, Liz Whiteside, Daniel Kramoris, the Benedictine Sisters of St. Joseph, Minnesota, the Reverend Jane Brady and Grace Church, Mayor Harold Griffin, Tim and Sally Ann Quinlan, Norma Ward, Bonnie Haines, Robin Mosher, Terry Jerome, Stacy Stockton, Damian Miller, Dee, Walter P. Knake Jr., all of the animals who have graced my life: Topaz, Elko, Obi, Timmy, Marlon, Pearl, Minnie, Salem, Lucky, Tiny and all the other rescues, Miss Precious, Jellybean, Euclid and any animal and person who is in my heart and who I am forgetting—I am very forgetful, and I apologize. Grateful acknowledgment is made to the Creator for keeping me going, and to the state of New Jersey, especially Pemberton, with its beautiful creative energy, and to this universe for all of its many gifts—thanks for all of it—I have been very lucky and blessed. Thanks to all of my students and all of my teachers, and to everyone who's ever crossed my path or will.